COYOTES IN THE CROSSWALK

Canadian Wildlife in the City

DIANE SWANSON

Illustrations by
DOUGLAS PENHALE

Whitecap Books
Vancouver/Toronto

Edited by Bruce Obee
Cover and interior design by Warren Clark
Cover and interior illustrations by Douglas Penhale
Printed and bound in Canada by D.W. Friesen and Sons Ltd.,
      Altona, Manitoba

Third printing, 1997

Canadian Cataloguing in Publication Data
      Swanson, Diane, 1944-
         Coyotes in the crosswalk
         Includes index.

         ISBN 1-55110-140-8
         1. Urban fauna—Canada—Juvenile literature.
      I. Penhale, Doug. II. Title.
      QL49.S93 1994   j591.971   C93-091953-x

The publisher acknowledges the assistance of the Canada Council and the Cultural Services Branch of the government of British Columbia in making this publication possible.

Contents

At Home in the City

There are coyotes in the crosswalk and frogs in the swimming pool...skunks waddling through churchyards and falcons diving off skyscrapers. With all its many buildings, streets and parks, the city may be home to people, but it is also home to wildlife.

Having wildlife in the city is not something new. Pigeons nested on houses and temples more than 6000 years ago. What's new is the study of the wildlife that lives in the city. It was the 1960s before scientists saw the city as a unique ecosystem—a place where living things affect each other and their surroundings in a special way. Now we are just beginning to learn how animals, including people, live together in the city.

City Life

The city provides many kinds of homes where animals can nest, rest, escape harsh weather and hide from their enemies. Bridges, billboards and buildings—from sheds to high-rises—are some of the things animals perch on, snuggle in or burrow under. Many parks, golf courses, schoolyards, cemeteries and neighbourhoods offer small "forests" of trees and shrubs. Backyards provide hideaways in rockeries, compost boxes and stacks of firewood.

When animals move into the city—or rove within it—they need safe places to travel and rest. They may follow railway tracks or move among bushes and trees that line roads or divide highway lanes. Once in town, some animals travel secretly through underground pipes connecting neighbourhoods. Some cities also have subway tunnels or wooded ravines that animals follow.

There is an almost endless supply of water and food in the city. Lakes in parks, ponds in yards and sprinklers on lawns are some of the places animals drink. And gardens, garbage and grocery stores

Critter Crossing

S pring-fed ponds and plenty of food were attracting herons, ducks, otters and raccoons to a neighbourhood in Saanich, British Columbia. But cars were hitting slow-moving ducklings and young raccoons as they crossed a busy road. One woman in the neighbourhood painted up some special crossing signs. Then she posted them on the street to warn drivers to watch for the animals.

provide plenty of food. Many city animals also prey on other city animals, like insects and mice. They don't have to compete for food and water with as many different animals as they would in the country. City animals don't have to travel as far to get food, either.

Despite the traffic, which kills lots of wildlife, city animals face fewer dangers than their country cousins. Hunting and shooting are not allowed in cities. People use smaller amounts of pesticides in cities than they do at many farms and orchards. And some of the animals who move to cities leave behind many of the country animals who eat them.

Cities also differ in climate. Their buildings block winds that sweep across the country. But some streets channel the wind, causing "wind tunnels," and tall buildings often cause updrafts.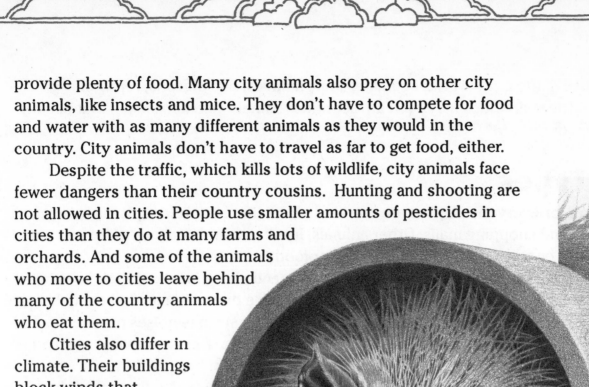

Most cities are warmer than the country, both day and night. Buildings and roads hold the heat that comes from the sun, and traffic, machinery and factories create more heat. At night, cities release heat more slowly than the countryside does.

The warm air often makes city skies cloudier—and that leads to more rain and snow. At least five to ten per cent more moisture normally falls in the city than in the country.

Because of the city's warmer climate, some animals, like pigeons, reproduce throughout the year. Cities may even attract other animals, like opossums, that usually live farther south.

City Types

City life isn't for everyone. Wolves are one kind of wildlife that prefers places far from traffic lights and shopping malls. Other animals, like bears and cougars, often just pass through cities or wander in and out, looking for food.

Still others adapt well, have their young and spend all, or much, of their lives in the city. They are usually animals that are smaller than large dogs and can find enough space in the city. They are also animals not easily frightened by strange noises or objects. And many of them are most active at night when cities are least busy.

Above all, city animals are flexible. Most eat many types of foods: plants and animals—living or dead. They are also willing to try new foods, like watermelon and pizza. They feed on things that are easy to find in cities. Birds, for instance, feast on insects that are attracted to street lights.

City animals accept different—often unnatural—homes. Bats rest in attics and church spires instead of hollow trees and caves. Magpies make nests in construction cranes; chimney swifts, in chimneys.

One of the most successful city animals is the house sparrow. It never seems to mind the hustle and bustle of the city and it eats many different foods. It nests anywhere from neon signs to drain pipes, and often builds its nest with lots of "city stuff," like string, paper, cellophane and rags.

Last Minute Mice

Travellers waiting for subway trains in Toronto, Ontario, can spot lots of mice. The animals scurry along dark track lines, nibbling crumbs of food. But they know when to take a break. As the train speeds into the station, they scamper off the track. Just in time, they duck into nooks and crannies on either side or dive under the rails themselves. As soon as the train pulls out, these city-wise mice are back, rummaging for food again.

The Starling is Ringing

Some birds make loud noises to scare their enemies. The starling, a songbird that lives in most cities in Canada, often imitates the calls of bigger birds. It also copies the barking of dogs and the meowing of cats. Even more startling are the sounds it imitates on downtown city streets: the shrieking of car burglar alarms and the ringing of portable telephones.

Scientists think that animals that live in the city will become even better at it in 50 to 100 years. And some think that people should learn to adapt to the animals. That doesn't seem easy when raccoons raid the garden and skunks dig holes in the lawn. But as scientists learn more about city ecosystems, they may find ways to help people and animals live together with less trouble.

Peregrine Falcons
The Skydivers

A blur is all you might see of the peregrine falcon. It's one of the fastest-moving animals on Earth. When it flies, it reaches speeds up to 100 kilometres an hour; when it skydives, it travels almost three times that fast.

Circling high in the sky, the peregrine falcon appears as a dark shape with long, pointed wings. But up close, it's a handsome bird—the size of a crow—with big brown eyes, a pale blue bill and black patches that form a "moustache" across its white cheeks.

There are few peregrine falcons in the world today, but they appear on all continents, except Antarctica. Some travel between continents, even flying over open stretches of ocean where they sometimes rest on ships. Many of the falcons that spend summer in Canada travel as far as Central and South America for winter. In fact, peregrine falcons were named for their wandering ways: "peregrine" means wanderer.

Hunting from the Heights

In the wilderness, peregrine falcons perch on high cliffs so they can scan the sky for prey. In cities, they use tall buildings for the same reason. From roofs, ledges—even the tops of large signs—on downtown skyscrapers, the falcons hunt birds, like pigeons, doves, ducks, sparrows and starlings. Falcons are attracted to cities because so many of these birds live there.

At dusk and dawn, the peregrine falcon begins its hunt. Even in the dim light, it sees so well it can spot a pigeon a kilometre away. The falcon normally uses its perch as a lookout but sometimes it circles the sky to search for food. It prefers to hunt sick or weak birds that are easier to catch.

As soon as it spots prey, the peregrine falcon charges into action. It may chase after its prey in flight, but more likely, the falcon prepares to dive. From a great height, it flaps its mighty wings, then holds them partly closed and plunges head-first. It falls like a thunderbolt—straight towards the target. Half-closed feet form fists that strike the prey with a thud heard for hundreds of metres. Then sharp claws and wide-spread toes grab the prey, usually still in the air. If the blow fails to kill, the peregrine falcon uses a toothlike point on its bill to pierce the prey's neck.

Sometimes a pair of peregrine falcons hunts as a team. One falcon flies low to flush prey out of hiding; the other waits up high, ready to dive on it.

Eggs in a Tray

In 1936, a pair of peregrine falcons swooped into downtown Montreal, Quebec. They landed on a building ledge 20 storeys above a busy street. People set trays of sand and gravel on the ledge, and the falcons began nesting and raising their chicks in the trays. Every year for 16 years, the same female returned to the same building. In all, she laid 50 eggs and raised 22 chicks, setting a breeding record in Canada.

Peregrine falcons still nest in downtown Montreal on newer buildings that are even taller and closer to a river.

Attracting a Mate

Peregrine falcons use their amazing flying and acrobatic skills to attract mates. The male may circle up high, zoom through several figure eights, then roll over and over. Then he may zigzag his way down, or swoop down and soar right up again.

Sometimes the male flies with the female he is courting. Together, they soar in circles and dive at each other in play. Often they roll over as they pass, occasionally grasping feet or touching bills—what some scientists call "aerial kissing." First one falcon, then the other may dive at great speeds, then shoot back up—a spectacular sight.

Peregrine falcons also court each other on their perch. Sometimes both birds hold their heads low. They point their bills down and bow to each other many times, wailing and making creaky-sounding calls. The male also presents food—like a gift—to the female.

Falcon mates normally stay together for life, and each year, they try to return to the same area to breed. They have one of the largest territories of all birds, usually settling more than a kilometre away from the nearest falcons.

Raising Chicks

Peregrine falcon mates not only return to the same territory each year, they try to return to the same nesting site. They prefer a spot that is close to water and safe from enemies, like great horned owls that eat falcon eggs and chicks.

In the city, nesting sites are often ledges on the upper storeys of tall buildings. Unlike many birds, peregrine falcons don't build nests; the female simply lays three or four reddish-brown eggs usually on a rough or carved ledge where they won't roll off. Then she sits on them for about a month. The male sometimes cares for the eggs but mostly he hunts to feed his mate and himself. Later he also hunts to feed the fluffy white chicks, which hatch with appetites as big as their oversized feet. In one day, they can double their weight.

Young peregrine falcons can learn to hunt on their own, but they seem to learn more easily with adults. When the young falcons are flying, their parents pass by with prey in their feet. The young try to snatch it. They get better and better at taking the food, even turning upside down beneath the parent birds to grab it.

The young falcons also learn by playing games together. They chase one another, then soar, circle and dive, pretending one of the young falcons is prey. Sometimes one will grasp the other's feet as they fly close together.

Soon their play involves other birds. At first, young peregrine falcons just pretend to attack, then they start to hunt for real. Before long, they can feed themselves; a couple of years later, they can support a family of their own.

Between the 1940s and the 1960s, the number of peregrine falcons in Canada dropped sharply. Pesticides—mainly one called DDT—in falcon prey made their eggshells very thin. When females tried to keep their eggs warm, the shells cracked. Canada seriously limited use of DDT in 1970 and banned it in 1990. But falcons still contact it in countries where they spend winter.

To produce more peregrine falcons, biologists breed some in cages and transfer their young to the wilderness and big cities. As a result, the population of peregrine falcons has been growing. If we're lucky, we will be able to spot these spectacular skydivers in Canada's skies for many years.

Falcon Foster Parents

A pair of peregrine falcons regularly nests in Calgary, Alberta—usually on the 14th floor of the telephone company building, close to a river. There, on a gravel ledge, they raise their own chicks plus a few "foster" chicks. Biologists take eggs—and sometimes, chicks—from caged falcons and give them to these wild falcons to look after. It's part of a Canadian program to increase the number of wild peregrine falcons.

When the falcons are nesting on the building, the telephone company puts a camera near the ledge. That way people in the building's lobby, at city hall or at Calgary's zoo can watch the birds on TV sets. Downtown shoppers and workers also watch the sky to see the young falcons learn to fly and hunt. One of the birds surprised crowds of people by landing on the road in the middle of the Calgary Stampede parade.

Raccoons
The Handy Ones

Raccoons are the handiest animals. Their paws are a lot like people's hands: each has a flat, bare sole and five, slender toes arranged like fingers. The sense of touch in their small front paws is especially keen. City raccoons use these paws to do a surprising range of things: untie string, open fridges, yank out door and window screens, unscrew jars, break glass with rocks, unhook gates—even turn on taps. When they want to get into something, raccoons are quick to learn how and slow to forget.

Found only in North and Central America, the raccoon is one of the few medium-sized wild animals that can live among people—and it lives very well. Raccoon numbers have grown particularly fast in cities, where there is plenty of food and shelter and few enemies. Thousands live in big centres, like Toronto, Montreal and Vancouver, and smaller populations live in other cities across southern Canada, except in Newfoundland.

The city raccoon usually grows to be heavier than its country cousin. But it sports the same ringed tail and the same black "mask" across its eyes and nose. The raccoon wears a warm, often brownish-grey coat that is really two coats in one. There's an inner layer of soft, thick wool and an outer layer of long, smooth hair that sheds water and keeps out the wind.

Feeling Right at Home

Raccoons settle comfortably into parks, cemeteries and treed neighbourhoods, especially close to water. But they avoid large open areas, such as soccer fields. If they want to move safely from one part of town to another, they often travel through culverts, pipes, and corridors of trees and bushes. On their short legs, they just waddle, but if chased, they can run up to 24 kilometres an hour for small stretches. Then they usually head for a tree.

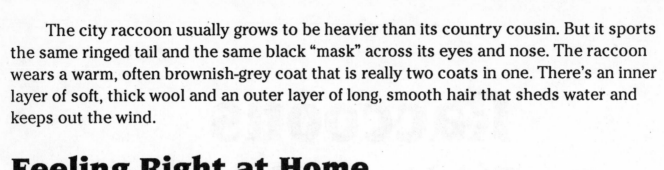

Raccoons feel more at home in trees than they do on the ground. With sharp, curved claws and widespread toes, their handy paws are great for climbing—and for hanging upside-down from branches. Their bushy tails help them balance when they run along branches. Their back feet, which can turn sideways, help them run down trunks head-first. Raccoons can also jump down to the ground without hurting themselves.

A high tree branch is a favourite place for a snooze, but most raccoons have several sleeping spots. Many like hollow trees, woodpiles, openings among rocks or dens dug by other animals. Some climb up fire escapes to the roofs of apartment or office buildings, rip the screens off vents and rest inside. Others prefer garages, sheds, greenhouses, churches, the attics or crawl spaces of houses, or the houses themselves—if no one is living there. Raccoons enter houses through chimneys or skylights and bed down in cozy places under cabinets or inside pianos.

Curled up in a ball or sprawled on its back—paws over eyes—the raccoon sleeps much of the day. In the winter, it also sleeps through most of the cold weather, heading out on pleasant nights to grab a snack.

Living Hand to Mouth

Variety is what raccoon meals are all about. Corn on the cob is a favourite

Raccoon City

With its very large raccoon population, Toronto is known as the "raccoon capital of North America." Even still, one Torontonian was amazed to be awakened inside the house by a mother raccoon and five young raccoons parading across the bottom of the bed.

Just how raccoons get into places can be a mystery. One was living in the rafters of a Toronto garage, where the door was always kept closed. No one could find any hole the raccoon might use to get in and out. Then one day, a man saw it in action: it simply pushed the button that opened the garage's electric door.

food, but raccoons also eat lots of other things: fruits, berries, nuts, seeds, grains, beetles, grasshoppers, crickets, hornets, worms, slugs, snails, birds, rabbits, mice, snakes, lizards, turtles, frogs, fish, crayfish, goldfish, crabs, mussels, oysters, clams— even pet food, ice cream cones and garbage. They seem willing to taste new foods and eat anything, except raw onions.

Raccoons that live along coasts eat mostly seafood. Others often hunt along rivers and streams, wading and swimming for their meals. Or they poke under stones and into tree stumps and burrows, using their sensitive paws to feel for food. Sometimes, they steal from gardens, kitchens, grocery stores and restaurants.

When raccoons find something to eat, they usually sit on their back legs and use their front paws and noses to check it over. For years, people thought that raccoons washed their food before eating it. But it seems that raccoons just soften their food by working it around in their paws underwater. Even when there is no water, raccoons frequently soften their food so they can tear it more easily.

Just Being a Kit

Tucked safely into a hideaway, like a hollow tree, the female raccoon gives birth to five or six fuzzy kits in spring. Each one weighs less than a bar of soap. The mother licks them clean, keeps them warm and lets them drink milk from her body.

When she leaves the den to feed herself, she stays close to hear the kits. If she thinks they are threatened, she may move them to safety. Using her teeth, she can carry each one by the skin behind its neck.

By the time the kits are three weeks old, they can open their eyes. Black hairs that form the rings on their tails and the masks on their faces start to appear. For the first time, they look like raccoons.

About six weeks later, the kits start to take short trips. One after the other, they walk behind their mother, watching what she catches and how she eats. Usually they walk at night, but if there is lots of food during the day, they may eat then.

All the while, the raccoon mother guards her kits. She hisses and snarls at enemies, ready to fight fiercely if she

Keeping Cosy

Raccoons in Winnipeg, Manitoba, have been living well for years. Raiding gardens and garbage cans, they find plenty to eat. They also manage to find cosy spots to escape Winnipeg's cold winters.

In one house, several lively raccoons had lived in the attic for four years. Finally, the owners called for help to move the animals. They had decided "enough was enough" when they discovered two young raccoons curled up in the fireplace.

must. She even keeps away adult male raccoons, which sometimes try to eat the young. But by fall, when the kits are about six months old, they can look after themselves. They usually stay with their mother through the winter, then begin their own adventures in spring.

Despite the dangers from coyotes, owls and traffic, raccoons enjoy a good life in the city. Most of them never come into contact with people. But those that do sometimes get in trouble because they are so "handy." Homeowners don't like the damage they can do and the mess they can make. Still, raccoons seem to be in the city to stay, so it's important that people and raccoons learn to get along.

Cottontails
The Multipliers

Rabbits don't do arithmetic but they multiply fast. Some females start breeding when they are just two months old. Then they breed again soon after they give birth. In a year, they can produce six litters of five or more rabbits each. As the young multiply, it's possible for a family of two to become a family of several hundred in only a year. However, most wild rabbits don't live that long, so their families don't grow as large as that.

Rabbits live all around the world, except in Antarctica. Canada's most common wild rabbits are cottontails, named for their tails, which look like fluffy balls of white cotton when they are held up. People often see cottontails in southern parts of British Columbia, Alberta, Saskatchewan, Manitoba, Ontario and Quebec.

These rabbits don't need much space so some live comfortably in the city—in places like gardens, cemeteries, parks and hospital grounds. Sometimes other rabbits, bred from European rabbits to live with people, also survive on their own in the city.

Cottontails are small rabbits—smaller than cats. Their fur is mostly grey or brownish-grey. It stays the same colour all year but it is thicker and longer in winter. Compared to many animals, cottontails have big ears, but compared to other kinds of rabbits, cottontail ears are quite short.

Growing Up a Cottontail

Before a female cottontail gives birth, she prepares a shallow nest—often on the ground beneath some bushes. She digs a small hollow just big enough to hold her young but not herself. She yanks out some soft fur from her underside and uses it to line the nest. Removing this fur also uncovers her nipples so her young can drink her milk easily.

At birth, cottontails are furless, sightless and helpless. They are no longer than a nail file. Their mother stands over them so they can drink her rich milk. When she has to leave the nest to feed herself, she covers it with fur and grass that helps to hide the young and keep them warm.

Cottontails change very fast. At one week, they can open their eyes. At two weeks, they can run—they are twice their birth size. At only three weeks, they can leave their nest and their mother. They are ready to take care of themselves.

Thriving Threesome

In 1965, the owner of a farm in Metchosin, on Vancouver Island, British Columbia, brought three young cottontails from Ontario. He put the rabbits in a cage for people to see but they escaped.

The two females and one male survived well on their own and, of course, they multiplied. As their numbers grew, the rabbits spread out. Today, people find these cottontails nibbling garden lettuce and broccoli in communities all over southern Vancouver Island.

Staying Safe and Warm

Lots of city animals like to eat cottontails: owls, raccoons, skunks, dogs, cats—even crows, which attack the young. But like all rabbits, cottontails have keen senses that warn them when enemies are near. Their long ears hear the softest sounds, and their sensitive noses pick up scents. Set far apart, their large eyes see in many directions.

When they sense danger, cottontails may thump their big back feet, drumming the ground to warn others. Or they may bound off, their long back legs covering about two bicycle-lengths in a single leap. For short stretches, the rabbits can travel more than 30 kilometres an hour.

Cottontails leave the most unusual trail. Their back feet strike the ground ahead of their front feet. They zigzag to make themselves hard to catch—and their scent hard to follow. They double back, or circle about, and return to their starting place. Along the way, they might even leap into water. Like all rabbits, cottontails can swim, but they would rather not.

Sometimes bounding cottontails suddenly screech to a halt. They squat low, tails down, and remain very still. Any enemies chasing the "balls of white cotton" would be confused: the topsides of the rabbits' tails—coloured the same as their backs—are much harder to spot.

Comforting Cottontails

The large, grassy area around a hospital in Victoria, British Columbia, is home to many rabbits. Some are cottontails; others are rabbits that were abandoned by their owners. Behind the hospital buildings, the rabbits find lots to eat and they entertain many patients and their visitors, who sit by the windows to watch them.

"The rabbits are wonderful to have around," said one of the nurses. "When people are sick, animals seem to raise their spirits."

Sometimes cottontails crawl into shelters: skunk burrows, openings among rocks or wood piles, hollow tree stumps, drain pipes and pieces of junk—like car parts. There they can escape their enemies and bad weather. Although cottontails do not sleep through the winter, they hide away to avoid storms and heavy snowfall. But when the weather is calm, they often rest in shallow holes that they dig in the dirt or the snow.

Eating All Year

As day ends, cottontails head out for a meal—often following paths and roads, where moving is easiest. In winter, they eat tree bark and twigs, sometimes licking the snow for moisture and the roads for salt. But in summer, they prefer green food, like grass, clover and young leaves. They love to hop into gardens to steal lettuce, cabbages, beans, peas and carrots. They even eat prickly plants, like raspberry and blackberry bushes. Standing on tiptoe, they can reach the tall branches, pulling the tender tips close enough to nibble.

The rabbit's sharp front teeth make great cutting tools. In a year, they would grow twice as long as a toothpick if the rabbit didn't wear them down. Its teeth are so much like rat teeth that people used to think rabbits were rodents. But rodents have only four front teeth; rabbits have an extra pair that grows right behind their top, front two teeth.

After the cottontail slices off some food with its front teeth, it chews it up with its back teeth. Its jaws move crosswise as it eats. That's what makes its nose twitch.

Then it's time to wash up. But the cottontail washes more than its paws. It washes everything, using its freshly licked front paws to help clean hard-to-reach places, like the back of the head and behind the ears. No matter how many cottontails you see, you aren't likely to find a grimy one.

Canadian cottontails are often hunted for food and sport, but in the city they are safe from shooting. Their biggest threats come from other city animals and from cars—headlights confuse cottontails.

These quiet rabbits often feed in backyards and many people enjoy having them around in the city. Some homeowners plant a little extra in their gardens, just for the cottontails.

Coyotes
The Super Adapters

Bigger than a fox but smaller than a wolf, the bushy-tailed coyote is the most adaptable dog in North America—the only place on Earth that it lives. If you change the food supply, the coyote changes what it eats. Build a city and the coyote moves right in.

Today, most wild animals live in fewer regions than they once did, but coyotes live in even more. As people removed forests and left fewer homes for the coyote's main enemy, the wolf, the coyote expanded its territory. In Canada, coyotes lived on the Prairies and in southern British Columbia in the early 1800s. A hundred years later, they were also in Ontario, Quebec and the northern territories. By the 1960s, they had reached the east coast.

When coyotes settle into a new area, they can triple their population there within a year. As individuals, they also do well—even in back alleys, empty lots and golf courses of big cities. In fact, city coyotes often grow larger than country coyotes because city eating is so good.

Chow Time

It's easy for coyotes to feed in the city. They are not fussy eaters. Coyotes steal food, like watermelons and cantaloupes, from crates behind stores. They raid gardens, digging under—or climbing over—tall fences to get seeds, vegetables and fruit. They follow dairy trucks and drink milk from cartons left on doorsteps at dawn. They even pick through leftovers in neighbourhood garbage cans, or eat dead animals.

Coyotes also hunt almost all the other animals that live in cities, including mice, rats, squirrels, small dogs, cats, rabbits, skunks, raccoons, birds, snakes, lizards, fish, frogs, turtles—even insects. Coyotes depend mostly on a keen sense of smell to sniff out prey. They also use their sharp ears to hear small animals that creep through the grass. Keeping their slim bodies near the ground, coyotes sneak up on their prey, then pounce. They can leap a distance more than twice the length of a bed.

If they have to chase their prey, coyotes can run 40 kilometres an hour and, in short bursts, 65 kilometres an hour. Besides being swift runners, coyotes twist and turn quickly, using their long tails for balance. Although they usually hunt alone, one coyote may chase an animal, like a rabbit, towards another coyote hiding under a bush.

Coyotes swim well and they dive into ponds or streams to catch water life, like crayfish. They also stick their heads underwater to nab fish with their teeth.

Sometimes a coyote will wait for food to come its way. It may pretend to be dead until an animal, like a crow, hops close enough for the coyote to snatch. Or it may wait while a badger digs into a ground squirrel's den, then catch the squirrel that runs out the back way.

Midnight Snack at the Golf Course

Y ou might not head to the golf course when you get hungry, but coyotes in Vancouver, British Columbia, often do. It's a choice spot for hunting mice and squirrels. And at night, coyotes have the place to themselves.

Another favourite place is the city's huge Stanley Park, home to many squirrels and rabbits. Coyotes travel along a beach to get to the park, coming and going in the early morning and evening.

Song Time

Coyotes are mostly night creatures so people seldom see them. But coyote "songs" often fill the skies, especially at dawn and dusk. Of all North America's land mammals, coyotes are the most vocal. That's why scientists named them *Canis latrans*, which means "barking dog."

People often hear one or two coyotes howling, then another howling back. A coyote may also answer the howl of a wolf or a dog. In the city, it may even answer the "howl" of car horns and sirens.

Like you, a coyote uses different sounds to mean different things. And depending on whether it wants to reach coyotes nearby or far away, it makes short or long distance calls, like these:

Short distance calls

- a growl or a huff to threaten
- a woof to threaten or alarm
- a yelp (yi-e-e-e) to alarm
- a "woo-oo-wow" or a whine to greet

Long distance calls

- a bark or a bark-howl to threaten or alarm
- a howl to contact or respond
- a yip-howl to greet or contact

Coyotes seem to know which howls come from others in their families. A howl from one coyote may mean: "I'm over here." Another coyote may howl back to say: "Well, I'm over here." Then the two can get together. Coyotes also howl at the same time. Often it's like a group cheer—a way to say: "We're glad we have each other." Just before coyotes go off to hunt, they may make a yip-howl. Sometimes it includes sounds like laughs or screams.

Puppy Time

If your mother were a coyote, you would likely be one, too—but you might be a "coydog" or a "coywolf," instead. Sometimes a female coyote breeds with one of her close cousins, the dog or the wolf. Then the pups are mixtures of two different animals. The first search-and-rescue "dog" used in Canada's national parks was a coydog, a German shepherd-coyote cross, named Ginger.

A female coyote usually produces one litter of about six pups in a year. They are born hairless and helpless. They can't even open their eyes for two to three weeks. Their mother stays with them in a den—often a hollow tree, a dirt dugout or an old skunk or badger burrow. Their father drops food for them at the entrance to the den. He hunts in the territory that he and his mate had claimed for their own.

As soon as the pups can see, they start spending time outside the den. Then both parents hunt to feed them. When the pups are about two months old, they begin to hunt for themselves.

Coyote pups, like dog pups, spend lots of time playing. They pretend to fight each other. They chase tails—their own and each other's. They run, jump and pounce on things—pebbles and whatever flutters, like leaves.

The family lives together for a few months, then the coyote pups usually head off on their own. They may mate and have pups when they are only a year old and stay with their mates for years.

Do You Hear What I Hear?

In New Brunswick in the late 1960s, people standing in their yards heard the yip-howl of the coyote and thought they were dreaming. Coyotes don't live in New Brunswick—at least they didn't until 1966. But as the number of cougars in Canada's eastern provinces fell, the ever-adaptable coyotes started to move in. By the 1970s, they had entered Nova Scotia. In the 1980s, they even managed to walk across frozen water and move into Prince Edward Island. Imagine what people there thought the first time they heard a yip-howl.

Many people fear coyotes and chill to the sound of their howls, but these wild dogs rarely attack humans. They may prey on small pets left outside, but they help people by controlling the numbers of mice, rats and rabbits in parks and neighbourhoods. And as one of the few larger wild animals that people may see close at hand, coyotes are something very special.

Common Garter Snakes
The Slitherers

With no legs—or even tiny bristles like earthworms have—it's surprising that the snake gets around at all. Yet it has ways of travelling that are unique among animals. The slender garter snake usually moves by twisting its body into several S-like curves. It presses the back of each curve against tiny bumps or hollows in the ground and slithers forward.

Of the 25 kinds of garter snakes in North America, one kind—called the common garter snake—lives from coast to coast in Canada, except in Newfoundland. And it lives as far north as the Northwest Territories. It even settles in large cities, living in parks, empty lots and backyards, especially near lakes and streams. It thrives among gardens, shrubs or rocks and in piles of firewood or junk. Sometimes it slithers into garages and basements, squeezing through slits or holes only as wide as a pencil.

Long, thin and usually striped, the common garter snake looks a bit like a type of garter that people once used to hold up their stockings. That's how the garter snake got its name. Its colour varies, but many common garter snakes are dark brown with yellow stripes or black with red stripes.

Warm Up, Cool Down

Garter snakes usually keep themselves cooler than your body temperature and warmer than room temperature. But they hardly produce any heat themselves. Instead, the snakes take what they need from warm objects and the air around them. Often they lie in the sun—on sun-heated rocks or cement—to warm up, then move into shade to cool down.

As fall days get shorter, it's harder for common garter snakes to get the heat they need. That's when they usually start heading to dens, like empty burrows or rock piles. Some snakes return to the same den each year, even travelling several kilometres over several days to get there.

All winter, temperatures in dens stay above three or four degrees Celsius— warm enough to keep garter snakes alive but too cold to allow them to be active. So the snakes hibernate: their breathing and heartbeats slow down, and they sleep deeply for months. They don't even wake to eat; instead, they live on fat stored in their bodies.

Snake as Big as a House

"The snake was so big its head came out the front door before its tail went in the back door," said a little boy in Kanata, Ontario. "It filled the whole house."

His friends were amazed until they realized he was talking about a dollhouse. Still, there was an amazing part to this story—not how big the snake was but how small it could make itself. The garter snake had squeezed into a basement through a slit narrower than the boy's finger. Then it "toured" the dollhouse until it was discovered and returned to a nearby creek.

Where winters are very cold, common garter snakes need very deep dens to escape freezing temperatures. If there are few dens that are deep enough, hundreds—even thousands—of garter snakes may need to share one.

In spring, it takes several warm days to heat up a den. Then the snakes gradually become active and begin to mate. In very large dens, a hundred males may try to mate with one female, forming a big, squirming ball of snakes.

Many kinds of snakes hatch from eggs. But garter snakes develop inside their mother where it is easier for her to control their temperature. They simply warm up and

Snake Capital

The people of Inwood, Manitoba, claim to live in the snake capital of the world. They say that, some years, they can't walk down the street without stepping on garter snakes. They say that they may even have to sweep the snakes off their front steps.

Twice each year, thousands of common garter snakes pass through Inwood on their way to or from their deep hibernating dens—several limestone pits near the town. As many as 15 000 snakes have spent the winter in one of these pits—the largest gathering of snakes in the world.

cool down as she warms and cools her own body. That's one reason garter snakes are able to live in so many climates—especially cold ones.

By late summer, the female garter snake gives birth to 20 or 30 young, each wrapped in a see-through sac. The number partly depends on the size of the mother. When they break out of their sacs, the young look just like little adult snakes but with slightly bigger heads. Unlike many other animals, common garter snakes can care for themselves right from birth.

Grab and Gulp

The common garter snake doesn't eat every day. But when it wants food, it usually starts hunting as soon as it warms up in the morning. Meals range from frogs, toads and fish to earthworms and leeches. Now and then, the snake also grabs a bird or a mouse. During the heat of a summer day, it usually rests, then starts hunting again in late afternoon and early evening.

Snakes hear only very low-pitched sounds, but their skin and bones sense ground vibrations made by some prey. And although garter snakes don't have great eyesight, they see better than most snakes. More helpful for hunting, though, are the snake's keen senses of smell and taste. Like other snakes, the common garter snake has a special organ in the roof of its mouth that receives smells and tastes delivered by the tongue. That's why the snake constantly flicks its tongue out to the air and towards objects, then back into its mouth again.

When there's something to eat, the snake snaps it up and swallows it whole. Prey that is fatter than the snake is no problem. The common garter snake just spreads its jaws apart and stretches enough to take the prey in. Then sharp teeth that point backwards help move the prey to the throat where strong muscles shift it along to the stomach.

Off with the Old

The common garter snake has skin like elastic so it can expand to swallow large prey. Large, ridged scales, made of the same material as your fingernails, cover the skin completely. They help keep the body from drying out and act like shields to protect the snake.

At least twice a year, the common garter snake sheds its outer layer of skin. A young snake may shed every five or six weeks because it is growing fast. Its old skin soon becomes too small.

The snake produces a fluid between its old and new skin that helps separate them. Then it starts rubbing the sides of its mouth and top of its head against rocks or rough ground. Bit by bit, it wriggles forward until it slithers right out of its old skin. If the skin comes off in one piece, it forms a pale, inside-out copy of the snake that was.

Many animals attack quiet-living garter snakes: other snakes, skunks, coyotes, raccoons, hawks, rats, dogs and cats. Even crows grab them to peck out their large livers. Traffic kills many more, and people collect lots of snakes to sell as pets or research animals. Given all the enemies it has, it's a wonder that this slitherer still gets around—another of the city's super survivors.

Canada Geese
The Honkers

Trucks and cars honk their way through streets jammed with traffic. But the noise doesn't drown out the honking that fills city skies each spring and fall. Canada geese use their very strong voices to honk loudly to each other as they fly. It seems to help the geese stay together in large groups. On the ground, they sometimes honk to signal the start of a flight, to warn other geese of danger, or to scare intruders.

From the Arctic Ocean to Mexico, Canada geese are the most common wild geese in North America. Many of them spend at least part of the year in each province and territory in Canada. Now people have introduced them to countries in Europe, too.

Canada geese spend time on wild marshlands and distant rivers, but they also slip right into large cities. There they swim calmly among canoes and sailboats on busy lakes. They nibble bread crusts tossed by picnickers.

Most Canada geese have metre-long, grey-brown bodies with white bellies. Their heads and necks are black, but the cheeks and chins of each bird are marked with a wide, white band that makes the goose easy to recognize.

Family Ties

The Canada goose is a family goose. It chooses a mate to be its partner for life, and the two remain loyal to each other. If one is sick or injured, the other stays with it—even if that means leaving the flock or putting itself in danger.

After geese mate in the spring, the female builds a grass-and-twig nest on the ground near water. She lines it with down—soft, fluffy feathers plucked from her body—then lays four or five eggs. For about a month, she tends her eggs carefully, pressing against them to keep them warm.

Meanwhile, the male goose guards the nest from skunks, raccoons, coyotes, dogs— even people much bigger than he is. First, he threatens: with neck stretched, mouth open and wings spread, he hisses, honks and charges. If that fails to scare away an intruder,

the male goose attacks. He can run faster than most people and can strike hard, using his long, strong wings.

When the eggs are about to hatch, the male goose moves even closer to the nest. Both parents guard the yellow-and-brown goslings as they break out of their eggs. The mother shields them from the cold and they often snuggle together to keep warm.

Within a day after hatching, the mother goose calls the goslings out of the nest. They form a line and walk to the water with a parent guarding each end. As the geese swim and feed, the parents continue to protect the goslings from birds in the sky and large fish and bullfrogs in the water.

The family of Canada geese stays together all summer—wherever it goes. The young birds can't fly until they are about two months old; neither can the parents for most of this time. Adult geese lose their flight feathers about the time their eggs hatch and don't grow new ones for five or six weeks.

The Wascana Geese

E very year, Regina, Saskatchewan, hosts lots of Canada geese. They gather by Wascana Lake near the legislative buildings and the city's downtown streets. Some come for the summer; others stay all year. The lake is part of a huge park that is well used, so the geese are comfortable with people. In fact, young Canada geese that grow up in the park often run up to visitors, expecting food. They especially run to children, who feed them more often.

When fall arrives, most Canada geese head south to warmer weather. They stay together as families—the young, their parents, grandparents and other relatives. Several families often fly together; sometimes hundreds of families form a flock so large that it darkens the sky overhead when it passes.

Fine Flying Form

When Canada geese fly away in the fall—and return in the spring—they travel thousands of kilometres. They fly for many hours at a time, day and night, and head for the same area each season. Scientists think that geese use different clues to help them find their way. They watch for landmarks, like lakes and mountains. They use the sun and stars as guides. Geese also seem to respond, like a compass does, to the pull of Earth's magnetic field.

As they travel, the geese follow "pathways" in the sky that lead them over rivers, lakes and marshes. That way, the birds can find food and water when they rest. The geese also feel safer if they can sleep on water.

Most of the time, Canada geese fly as high as small planes, 300 to 900 metres above the ground. But they can fly much higher, easily crossing lofty mountain peaks. Their average flying speed is about 65 kilometres an hour. Winds blowing their way help them travel even faster, and if they are in danger, they can reach speeds of 100 kilometres an hour.

Flying together, Canada geese form a huge letter "V" across the sky. Researchers think that the bird at the front—the point of the "V"—breaks through the air and makes updrafts with its wings. The flock follows, each bird flying just behind and a bit to the side of the bird in front. Using updrafts made by the birds in front makes flying easier. Geese seem to fly almost twice as far if they form a "V" than if they fly on their own. But the geese must take turns doing the tough job of being the front bird at the point.

Not all Canada geese travel in the spring and fall. Some live all year in the same place—often at city parks, lakes and golf courses. Many of these geese had parents, grandparents or great-grandparents who couldn't travel because they were hurt. Then their young stayed with them. Living in one place became a way of life.

Celebrating "Wild Goose Jack"

Every October, the people of Kingsville, Ontario, honour the Canada goose by holding a special festival. They gather to watch thousands of geese take to the skies to fly south for the winter. They display bird carvings, paintings and crafts. They even hold a "Wild Goose Run," a six-kilometre race for runners and rollerbladers.

The Kingsville festival also celebrates the memory of Jack Miner, who set up one of the first bird sanctuaries in North America in 1908. "Wild Goose Jack," as he was called, lived in Kingsville but gave talks about the sanctuary all over North America and Europe. He inspired other people to care about wild birds.

Super Bills, Fabulous Feathers

The Canada goose is well equipped for the life it leads. When it pokes its head underwater, the sensitive tip of its bill feels for plants. The edges of the bill are ragged—like a bread knife—so the goose can strain out water when it has a mouthful of plants. On land, the Canada goose uses the sharp front of its bill to clip grass. It can even strip kernels of corn off their cobs.

Before it hatches, a gosling has a special tool on its bill: a hard, sharp bump, called an egg tooth. It uses this tooth to break through the eggshell, sometimes chipping away for a day and a half. The egg tooth drops off soon after.

The Canada goose also uses its bill to waterproof its feather coat. With the tip of the bill, it collects oil from a gland at the base of its tail. Then it spreads the oil onto many of its feathers.

The Canada goose has different kinds of feathers for different uses. The long, strong ones that edge its wings help the goose fly. And the soft, fluffy down beneath the outer layer of feathers keeps the goose warm. This same down helps goslings swim by making it easier for them to float.

Some cities welcome Canada geese; others think they are a nuisance. Yet the honking of a flock turns heads upwards and the "V" across the sky thrills onlookers. The sound and the sight of Canada geese bring a little bit of the wilderness home to the city.

Rats
The Survivors

In the 1940s—just after the Second World War—the United States tested some bombs by dropping them on tiny islands in the Pacific Ocean. The explosions flattened trees and blasted huge craters in the ground. They created poisonous clouds and giant waves, which flooded the land. Scientists thought nothing on these islands would live. But a few years later, they were amazed to find strong, healthy rats—hundreds of them. Not only had these rats survived the bombs, but they were living longer lives than rats normally do.

Rats live in every country on Earth and, worldwide, they outnumber people. In Canada, most rats are either black rats, which live on the west coast, or brown rats, which live in cities across much of the country.

Brown rats make their homes in old buildings, new buildings, backyards, junkyards, garbage dumps, empty lots, parks, harbours, subways and sewer pipes. Their many homes led to their many names: house rats, alley rats, earth rats, water rats, barn rats, sewer rats, dump rats, river rats and wharf rats. They are also called Norway rats because they came to North America from Norway and other parts of Europe. But most often, they are just called brown rats. That's because brown is their usual colour, although some—like the ones people keep as pets—are white.

Winning Ways

The brown rat has many skills that help it thrive in the city. From nose to tail tip, it is only a bit longer than a 30-centimetre ruler, but it can jump as high as a table and leap the length of a bathtub. It can also squeeze through a hole the size of a quarter. Although it doesn't climb as well as the black rat, the brown rat can move easily through pipes that run straight up and down. It can also run along telephone wires and power lines, using its hairless tail for balance. And it can swim—even underwater—and tread water for up to three days.

Although brown rats are all around, people seldom see them. They are mostly night animals that move under, through and between things. They pass beneath floorboards, scurry within walls and crawl through underground burrows. Brown rats cannot see well but their long whiskers help them feel their way. They also have a special "muscle sense" that helps them remember their way through contact with their surroundings.

Rats are quick to detect and avoid danger. They have a keen sense of smell that warns them of enemies, like cats. They often avoid traps that people set out, sometimes stealing the trap bait without getting caught. Rats also notice very tiny amounts of anything strange in their food, which makes them hard to poison.

If they need to, brown rats can fight. Sometimes they box each other by standing on their hind legs and using their front paws to strike. Their boxing often helps them decide who is more important within a pack of rats. If they are cornered, rats may even try to fight animals much larger than themselves.

Above all, brown rats thrive because they reproduce so well. Unlike many animals, rats mate all through the year, usually giving birth to five litters of nine to eleven rats each. When these young rats are just two or three months old, they start producing their own families.

Gnawing Hunger

Although brown rats can live two weeks without food, they like to eat lots and they eat almost anything: garbage, compost, clothing, leather shoes—even toenails on zoo elephants. But if they have a choice, rats eat well-balanced meals that include grains, vegetables, eggs, meat and fish. Sometimes they steal bird eggs from nests and dive into ponds to catch fish. Rats also eat mice and other rats.

Like people, rats need to drink water every day. They turn to puddles, ponds and garden hoses but they also drink the morning dew on grass and shrubs. If they have to, rats even gnaw through pipes to reach water.

The rat often chews to get what it wants. Its front teeth are strong and sharp enough to gnaw through plastic, wood, metal—even concrete. They always stay sharp and never stop growing. If the rat didn't keep wearing them down, its teeth would likely pierce its own head.

Hidden Hitchhikers

There's a rat patrol in Alberta—people who work to keep rats out of the province. The patrol sets traps and checks crates of goods coming into Alberta. Still, some rats manage to sneak in.

One year, rats from Saskatchewan slipped into a town on the Alberta border and hid inside empty cans and bottles. A truck picked up a load of these cans and bottles and took them to a recycling centre in Edmonton. Along went the rats. By the time they were discovered, they had bred, producing the first rats known to be born in Alberta for years.

Eating Like a Bird

One Christmas, a woman in Victoria, British Columbia, made a special treat for the chickadees that visited her yard. She drilled holes in a small log and packed it with suet, peanut butter and seeds. Then she hung it by a wire from an arch in her yard. That same day, she spotted her first visitor: a rat. It had climbed up the arch and was feasting on the treat.

Another woman in Victoria stuck a plastic bird feeder to the window of her den so she could feed the wild finches. To her surprise, a rat jumped up to the outside window sill and hopped boldly into the feeder. The next day, it even came back to eat up the birdseed it had scattered on the ground.

Home Sweet Home

Brown rats often make a home together. Fifteen to two hundred rats can share one underground burrow. They dig several tunnels in the burrow to join nesting areas with the places where they pile their food. They also make side tunnels to use for their toilets. Most burrows have several escape holes, which the rats hide with a layer of leaves or dirt.

When the brown rat gets tired, it may yawn and stretch—like you do. Then it curls up in the burrow, resting its head on its front legs. Usually, it sleeps for longer stretches during the winter than during the summer.

As soon as it wakes up, the brown rat cleans itself all over, starting with its front paws. It licks these paws, then uses them to wipe its face and head—even behind the ears. When the rat cleans its tail and hind legs, it holds them with its paws. Many times a day, the rat stops to groom itself.

The nests in the burrows are shaped like cereal bowls, only wider. Brown rats make them from soft things, like cloth, string, grass and leaves. Softness is important because

rats are born without any hair. They lie helplessly in the nests, barely able to move. They see and hear nothing for almost two weeks. Mother rats feed and care for their own and each other's young. But soon these young rats are ready to head into the city and hunt for themselves.

Rats will likely always share our cities. They cause problems, like damaging buildings and spreading some diseases, but they help solve problems, too. Since 1900, researchers have used rats in experiments more than any other animal. Many of these experiments have helped test new drugs and find cures for illnesses. People can learn a lot about surviving from rats, the survival experts.

Feral Cats
The Hunters

Thousands of years ago, all cats were wild animals. Gradually, some became domestic—tame enough to live with people. The pets we have today came from these early cats. But domestic cats can become wild again—or "feral." If they are lost or abandoned, those that manage to live survive by hunting. When they reproduce, their kittens never know a human home; they are wild animals.

Feral cats live in countries all around the world, including Canada. They thrive in large cities where there is lots of food, moving into places such as factories, warehouses, dockyards, sheds, sewers and underground garages. They appear in the same wide range of colours as domestic cats. But cats whose families have been wild for many years may grow larger and heavier.

Born to Hunt

The feral cat is a skilled, well-equipped hunter. Just like the domestic cat, it has a strong, but nimble, body with front legs that turn almost any direction and back legs built to spring and sprint. With superb balance, the cat climbs, walks narrow spaces—fences and railings—and lands on its feet when it leaps from rooftops. On feet like furry slippers, it walks soundlessly, but it can flick its claws out in an instant. The points of these claws—only exposed when needed—always stay sharp.

The cat hunts at night, seeing well in one-sixth the light that people need. It uses the fine sense of touch in each hair and whisker to feel in the dark. It detects the faintest smells. It swivels its outer ears to hear the scratching of a mouse paw or the high-pitched cry of a rat. The cat uses more than twenty muscles to swivel these amazing ears.

Having sensed its prey, the feral cat stalks it, creeping slowly from hiding place to hiding place. In open stretches, the cat presses its body flat against the ground. When it gets close to its prey, the cat crouches and stares. The tip of its tail twitches. Then all at once, the cat charges. It leaps into the air and pounces down on its prey.

The cat's jaws and sharp teeth are built to snatch. It can kill with a single bite, usually to the neck. Then it tears up its prey and uses its rough tongue to scrape meat from bones.

The feral cat hunts birds, squirrels, rabbits and fish, but in the city, rats and mice make up most of its meals. It avoids people but sometimes steals pet food from homes and eats garbage, such as vegetable peels and fish heads, from trash cans. Few feral cats live without taking any food from people's homes.

Gone Fishing

A woman in New Glasgow, Nova Scotia, lost her pet cat. After searching her neighbourhood, she called the animal control officer for help. That night, he suggested they check a small goldfish pond that he knew was popular with cats, both feral and domestic. When the woman and the officer arrived, they shone a flashlight around the rim of the pond. One hundred fifty pairs of eyes shone back—one hundred fifty cats were fishing for a midnight snack.

Kitten Care

Male feral cats usually live alone, but females often live with other females—probably their own, grown daughters. They rest in groups, groom each other's fur and raise their kittens together.

The feral cat usually gives birth to four or five helpless kittens in a "nest"—any small, sheltered spot. At first, the kittens stay together in a furry ball, the head of one nestled on the shoulders of the next. If a kitten rolls away, it can't find its way back. Its crying attracts the mother cat, who uses her teeth to pick up the kitten by the skin on its neck. If anything threatens the nest, the mother may move the whole litter, one by one. She checks carefully to make sure she leaves none behind.

When the kittens are about three weeks old, they begin to leave the nest for short times. The mother carries them back if they go too far. She keeps returning them to the nest even after the kittens have grown much heavier—but by then, she may have to drag them.

Until the kittens can run from danger, the mother cat is willing to attack almost anything that threatens them. And she fights especially fiercely. A few seconds is all she needs to pounce on a dog, beat it soundly with her paws and make it run off. The startled dog may return, but by that time, the cat will have hurried her kittens to safety. Her actions teach them to fear dogs and other cat-eating animals.

When the kittens are four weeks old, their mother starts bringing prey to the nest. A week later, the kittens may start catching mice, but until they are older and bigger, the mother cat won't let them chase rats. Gradually, they start hunting on their own.

Cat Talk

Cats can't speak words, but they have ways of "talking." A mother makes one kind of noise to tell her kittens she is bringing them a mouse, and a different noise if she has a rat. And the feral cat, like the domestic cat, may purr to court a mate or to say, "I'm relaxed. I'm feeling great." Kittens first purr when they are just a few days old—when they are drinking milk from their mother. That lets her know that they are feeling fine. She often purrs at the same time. Adult cats may also purr to say, "I'm not as important as you," which might prevent fights amongst them.

Cats use their bodies to talk, too. Glands between their ears and eyes produce oil that they rub on one another. The cat being rubbed is sometimes the more important one. Cats also use head rubbing when they court each other or when they just want to show they are friendly. Sometimes all the cats in the same group rub each other; then the oil is like a membership badge.

Other signs of friendliness include blinking when one cat stares at another. And when cats enter and leave a group, they regularly hold up their tails: it seems to be a way of keeping goodwill among the cats they see day to day.

Cats also stretch along tree trunks and other rough things and scratch with their front paws. It's thought that cats say several things this way, including, "I'm tougher and more important than you."

All cats in the city face the dangers of being chased by dogs, hunted by coyotes or struck by cars. But the feral cat doesn't have the protection of a home with people and no one sets out food for it. The feral cat survives as its wild ancestors did thousands of years ago—ever watchful and ever the hunter.

Red Squirrels
The Chatterers

A loud "tchrrrrr" from a nearby tree branch startles you. "Tchrrrrr!" You hear the cry again as you spot the flicking of a bushy tail and the stomping of two tiny feet. A small red squirrel—its body no longer than a table knife—is scolding you just for standing too close to its tree.

Noisy and bold, this small rodent is one of about 260 kinds of squirrels in the world. In Canada, there are six kinds of tree squirrels—in a range of sizes and colours—but the red squirrel is the one that lives in most parts of the country. In fact, its shrill cry and steady chatter are heard in every province and territory, prompting nicknames, like "boomer" and "barking squirrel."

During the summer, the red squirrel's soft fur is reddish-brown or grey, flecked with black. In the winter, it is redder and thicker. A black line that runs along each side of the squirrel in the summer fades away in colder weather. But all year, the squirrel's eyes are ringed with white.

Easy to Spot

Red squirrels are small, but they're not hard to find. That's partly because many of them live in cities, especially in parks, cemeteries and neighbourhoods that have lots of trees. Sometimes these squirrels even drop into houses by falling down chimneys. And they are active all day and all year. Storms force them to take cover, but as soon as the weather clears, they're out and about—even when it's well below freezing. Sometimes, in the fall, they also appear on moonlit nights to gather food.

Red squirrels have lots of energy and always seem to be dashing around. They are not as shy as many other kinds of squirrels. And living in the city has made them even bolder than their cousins in the forest. City squirrels often try to chase off anything—of any size—that comes near their trees.

Even if you don't spot a red squirrel, it will likely spot you. It is very watchful and quick to react, making about four different kinds of sounds. The noise often excites birds, like jays, which join in.

No Shocked Squirrels

Tree squirrels climb more than trees; they also scamper up city hydro poles. But there is a danger: high-voltage electricity can strike them, killing the squirrels and knocking out the power. Calgary, Alberta, is one city that has taken steps to protect squirrels—and birds, too. It puts plastic "wildlife protectors" on electric transformers. Besides saving lives, these protectors prevent the power from going out. And everyone is happier.

At Home in the Trees

Racing up tree trunks is easy for a red squirrel. It's designed for life among the trees. Small, agile feet with sharp, curved claws help it cling to tree bark. And a long, thick tail gives it balance as it races along branches. It can even run on the undersides of branches and charge, head-first, down trunks.

When it reaches the end of a branch, the red squirrel leaps off, stretching out all four feet. It may jump several metres across to the next tree or drop many metres to a lower branch. Even if the

squirrel falls from the top of a tree to the ground, it will likely land unharmed. It slows its fall by grasping branches on the way down and by "drifting" on its outstretched legs. Sometimes it travels by racing down one tree, galloping across the ground, then scampering up the next tree.

Red squirrels live in nests in trees. They sometimes fix up nests left by large birds, like owls or hawks. Or squirrels build their own nests in tree hollows, in holes made by woodpeckers or on thick, sheltered branches. They often shred leaves and twigs to build the nests, then line them with soft material, like fine bark. Then they crawl in at night to sleep. They also groom there, using their tongues to wash themselves and their teeth to comb their beautiful tails.

Usually in spring, female squirrels give birth in their tree nests. They raise litters of four or five young that begin life hairless and pink. By the time they are eight weeks old, the young squirrels dare to leave the nest and start exploring. After a few months, they head off to set up tree homes of their own.

Red on White

Skating on a frozen lake in Ottawa, Ontario, a boy stopped by a snowbank to tighten his laces. As he bent over, he heard a sharp cry. The sound scared him until he saw what had made it. The bright-eyed, furry head of a red squirrel was poking out of the snow, likely near one of its food piles. It kept shrieking until the boy skated away.

Squirrelling Away

Red squirrel food is whatever red squirrels find: insects, soil, small birds, eggs, mushrooms, dead mice from owl nests, salt off icy roads—even pizza and popcorn from garbage cans. They eat more meat, including bones, than other tree squirrels, and they drink more water, too. But red squirrels take most of their food from the trees: seeds, nuts, cones, flowers, fruit and bark. Sometimes, they also gnaw through the bark to lick sap from trees, like sugar maples and sweet birches.

When red squirrels harvest cones and seeds, they strip them right off the branches. They let the large cones from trees, such as pines, fall to the ground. Then they pile the cones up to a metre high in damp, shady places to keep them from drying.

All year long, red squirrels gather food. In the fall, they save some for winter. They store it beneath rocks, in holes in the ground, in hollow logs and among bushes. They may store three or four nuts at one spot, but several kilograms at another. They dry some food, like mushrooms, on tree branches before storing it away.

When snow buries the ground, red squirrels dig tunnels through it. That way they can travel safely from their nesting trees to their food piles. Squirrels have trouble remembering where they have hidden food, but their sense of smell tells them. They can sniff out nuts and seeds through snow and soil so deep it could bury a basketball. They rarely miss a meal.

Sometimes red squirrels bother people by raiding fruit trees or chewing outdoor wires, but they also help save evergreen trees by eating harmful insects. Besides, their excited chatter and frisky ways often cheer people in the city.

Striped Skunks
The Misunderstood

What a bad reputation the striped skunk has. People know it mainly for its smell—even scientists call it *Mephitis mephitis,* which comes from a Latin word, meaning "bad smell." Language also links the skunk with bad things: people use it to mean "someone who cheats" or "someone who is just plain disgusting."

It's true that striped skunks can make an awful stink. In fact, the stink can be so strong that people at sea smell it 30 kilometres from shore. But skunks don't often create a stink; some never do. Most of the skunks that people smell are those hit by cars and trucks. Skunks produce their awful-smelling oil mainly to defend themselves—and then, only as a last resort. And they never release it if they are likely to get it on themselves.

Related to weasels, badgers and otters, the striped skunk is only as big as a pet cat. It is a handsome animal with long, shiny fur and a soft, wavy undercoat. Usually it is black with a thin, white stripe from nose to forehead and two wide, white stripes along its back. The skunk's long, bushy tail may be trimmed with white. All together, the bold, black-and-white colouring acts as a warning that tells other animals: "Leave me alone…or else."

Striped skunks live only in North America; in Canada, they are in all provinces, except Newfoundland—unlike spotted skunks, which live only in part of British Columbia. In the city, striped skunks make homes in parks, empty lots and backyards, usually near water.

Hiss, Stomp, Fire

Short legs and flat feet do not help striped skunks escape danger. Their walk is more of a waddle. Two of their enemies—coyotes and dogs—run about four times faster than skunks do.

The striped skunk scares animals more easily than it outruns them. Facing danger, it raises its long hair to make itself look larger. It may arch its back, fixing its dark, round eyes on the enemy. The skunk may also march forward, growling and snarling.

If that's not enough to make the enemy run, the skunk carries on. It clicks its sharp teeth and hisses. It stomps its front feet furiously for minutes at a time. It raises its tail. Then it issues a final warning: it curves its body to the side so its head and rear end both point towards the enemy.

If the skunk still feels threatened, it may decide to launch the smelly oil produced by glands in its rear end. It can hit an animal that is up to four metres (two bed-lengths) away. The skunk takes aim, then fires. Oil shoots out through nipplelike openings in a steady stream or a fine spray—the skunk's choice. That's enough to make dogs and coyotes race off. The oil stings their eyes and skin and makes them feel sick for a short while. But this unique weapon is useless against great horned owls, which love skunk dinners.

Varied Menu

Insects are favourite items on a striped skunk's menu. They include lots of stinging insects, like bumblebees, hornets and wasps. Unlike people, the skunk does not suffer from stings. It just scratches hives and digs into nests, then grabs the insects that charge out. The skunk uses its front paws to kill them, rolling them against the thick skin of its soles.

The skunk catches beetles and grasshoppers by leaping on them. It also digs up insects under rocks, logs and lawns. Sometimes, a skunk may roll up a strip of lawn—like a rug—then dig for insects in the soil.

Striped skunks also eat many other kinds of food. They nibble grass, leaves, nuts and fruit. They steal bird eggs from nests on the ground. They snatch frogs, minnows and crayfish from the water. They hide and wait for some animals, like young rabbits, to pass by. Or, like cats, they stalk prey, such as rats and mice. Some skunks are better than cats at catching mice.

As daylight dims, skunks start searching for their food. They prefer to hunt close to home. Although they don't like the water, they can swim—even hours at a time—to reach good hunting grounds or avoid danger.

Striped skunks count on their keen sense of smell to help them hunt, sneezing often to clear their noses. They can even sniff out insects beneath the soil. Then the skunks dig them up, using long, curved claws on their front feet. Digging is something else that skunks do very well.

Ahh! Such Sweet Smells

Someone in Moose Jaw, Saskatchewan, loves the stink that skunks produce. What's more, this person is not alone. He or she responded to a newspaper ad that read: "Calling All Skunk Lovers! Reply if you like the scent of skunks." Within five weeks, 71 people in North America answered the ad. Several of them wrote that—as much as they love the smell of skunks—they don't like to admit it to their friends.

The Family Next Door

One day, a family in busy Montreal, Quebec, noticed another family living on the lot next to them. Nothing strange about that, except that the lot was "vacant"—and the family was furry. Under a tree on the lot lived a mother skunk with her four young, a small part of the city's growing skunk population.

From time to time, the human family spotted the skunk family heading out at night. The young skunks, called "kits," would walk in a single line behind their mother. When she stopped to sniff, poke and dig for insects, the kits stopped and watched. When she whistled softly, they hurried back into line, and they all headed off again.

Down in the Den

After searching for food all night, the striped skunk returns to its den to sleep. The den may be a hollow in a tree, woodpile or large rock, or one under a house, shed or garage. It may be a burrow that the skunk has dug in the ground or that some other animal has made. Whatever it calls home, the skunk usually lines it with a layer of grass and leaves.

Striped skunks often prefer to live above ground during summer and below ground during winter—and when a female has young. Although they often live alone, skunks may gather in numbers up to 24, just to keep warm in winter. Or they may share a den with other kinds of animals, like raccoons or rabbits. Skunks sleep through much of the cold winter, but they wake up if temperatures rise. Then they may leave their dens at night and hunt for food.

Misunderstood for years, these black-and-white beauties are not the stinkers they are often thought to be. Like all city wildlife, they just want a place to live, eat and raise their young. As their numbers grow, they are learning how to adapt to our ways. Perhaps it's time we learned how to adapt to theirs.

Acknowledgements

My warmest thanks go to:

- Michael McNall and David Nagorsen of the Royal British Columbia Museum, Patrick Gregory and Neville Winchester of the University of Victoria, and Barry Saunders of the British Columbia Ministry of Environment, Lands and Parks for their thoughtful reviews of chapters in this book;

- Keith Webb of the Inglewood Bird Sanctuary, Kathy Dolan of AGT, David Bird of McGill University and Ernie Demarse of the Kingsville Migration Festival for providing useful information;

- the diligent librarians of the Greater Victoria Public Library for their cheerful help in searching for out-of-the-way facts; and

- Douglas Penhale for the splendid artwork he completed specially for this book, and Carol Penhale for her help in coordinating the art with the text.

Index

About the Author

Diane Swanson lives on Vancouver Island, B.C. Her articles on nature and wildlife have appeared in children's magazines *Ranger Rick* and *Owl*. She is the author of five "Our Choice" children's books: *A Toothy Tongue and One Long Foot, Why Seals Blow Their Noses, Squirts and Snails and Skinny Green Tails, Coyotes in the Crosswalk,* and *Sky Dancers.* Diane Swanson is also the author of *The Emerald Sea,* and *Safari Beneath the Sea,* which won an Orbis Pictus Award for outstanding children's non-fiction.

About the Illustrator

Douglas Penhale is a freelance artist living on Saltspring Island, B.C. His avid interest in nature, together with a move to the West Coast, turned him from commercial art to wildlife illustration. His nature drawings and cartoons have been featured in many books and magazines, and he was the Grand Prize Winner at the International Cartoon Festival in 1985. Douglas Penhale has also illustrated *Why Seals Blow Their Noses, Sky Dancers,* and *The Coastal Birder's Journal.*